# Survey of Public Library Efforts to Provide Job Information Resources

ISBN: 978-1-57440-219-3
Library of Congress Control Number: 2012955708

# TABLE OF CONTENTS

# LIST OF TABLES

# THE QUESTIONNAIRE

## CLASSES AT THE LIBRARY

1. Does the library offer classes in any of the following subjects?

    A. Use of internet job boards
    B. General job search skills
    C. Resume writing
    D. GED or other high school equivalency classes
    E. Civil service exam preparation
    F. ESL (English as a Second Language)

2. Does the library offer classes in the use of any of the following social networks for job search purposes (or cover its use in general classes about job searches)?

    A. Facebook
    B. LinkedIn
    C. YouTube

## RESOURCES AND OTHER INSTRUCTIONAL MATERIALS

3. In the past year, how much did the library spend on books, CDs, instructional materials, eBooks, databases, and other materials specifically to address or equip the job center with reference and educational materials?

4. In the past year, how much did the library spend on books, CDs, instructional materials, eBooks, databases, and other materials specifically to address or equip the job center with reference and educational materials? Per full-time equivalent employee.

5. Name some of the most heavily used resources in your job information center or job related reference collection.

6. Does the library itself serve as a conduit for want ads or other advertisements of job availabilities either through a bulletin board, listserv, or other information device?

7. Has the library itself prepared a video or podcast on how to use the library's overall job-finding resources?

8. What materials or resources are you planning to purchase in the near future to enhance your job research information center or collection and why are you going to purchase such resources?

## THE JOB CENTER SPACE

9. How many visitors does the library's employment information center or reference collection attract in a typical week?

10. What has been the average annual percentage increase (or decrease) in such visitors over the past three years?

11. How has the library adjusted its workstation access policies to accommodate those doing job-related research?

12. Has the library ever held a job fair?

13. If the library has ever held a job fair, how many participants attended?

## PARTNERSHIPS

14. Has the library partnered with any of the following types of organizations to sponsor classes in job search skills or to otherwise offer job search related advice and information?

    A. Churches or other houses of religious worship
    B. Other non-profit organizations
    C. Unions
    D. K-12 schools
    E. Colleges
    F. Government agencies

15. If you have had cooperative relationships with other organizations in developing or supplying job search information or skills, please briefly describe these ventures.

16. Which phrase best describes the library's attitude toward the use of career coaches?

    A. We employ or contract one or more at the library to help patrons
    B. We will put patrons in touch a career coach or give them a list of coaches
    C. We don't really get involved in this at this point

## LIBRARY STAFF

17. About what percentage of reference library staff time would you say is taken up by assistance to job seekers?

18. Does the library have one or more persons specifically devoted to a job center or job center related activities?

19. Explain your personnel strategy for your jobs research effort. Do you have one or more specialists? Do you hire freelancers or contractors to teach classes in resume writing, internet job board use, interviewing skills, and other areas? What is your strategy and how do you deploy staff and other labor?

## ONILNE PRESENCE

20. Does the library job center have an online presence on any of the following locales that discusses and presents the job center's resources?

    A. Library website
    B. Local government website
    C. Library's LinkedIn page
    D. Library's Facebook page
    E. Library's Google+ page
    F. Library's YouTube page

21. Are there information sources such as websites, listservs, blogs, periodicals, conferences, or other resources that you have found useful in setting up and managing your job information center? If so, what are they?

## ASSESSMENT

22. Has the library developed any way to assess or track how its job search efforts help library patrons? Has it developed a database of stories by patrons who found jobs through the library or made some kind of similar efforts?

23. How useful a tool would you say that the library's job center or job reference effort has been in enhancing the library's local image and obtaining funding for the future?

24. What advice would you give to public libraries in setting up or managing a job information center?

# SURVEY PARTICIPANTS

Bellingham Public Library (Bellingham, MA)
Cheshire Public Library (Cheshire, CT)
Douglas County Libraries
East Baton Rouge Parish Library
German Historical Institute
Indian Valley Public Library (Telford, PA)
LaFollette Public Library (LaFollette, TN)
Laramie County Library System
Latah County Library District
Lawrence Library (Pepperell, MA)
Linebaugh Public Library (Murfreesboro, TN)
Mishawaka Public Library (Mishawaka, IN)
O'Kelly Memorial Library (Loganville, GA)
Patterson Library (Patterson, NY)
Perry County District Library
Shaker Heights Public Library (Shaker Heights, OH)
Sno-Isle Libraries
Southwest Wisconsin Library System
Spokane Public Library (Spokane, WA)
St. Mary's County Library
Upland Public Library (Upland, CA)
Westport Public Library (Westport, CT)
Williamson County Public Library
Wilmington Public Library of Clinton County

# CHARACTERISTICS OF THE SAMPLE

Overall sample size: 24

## By Type of Library

| | |
|---|---|
| Central library in a system | 7 |
| Entire library system | 13 |
| Branch library | 4 |

## By FTE Employees

| | |
|---|---|
| Less than 10 | 9 |
| 10 to 49 | 7 |
| 50 or more | 8 |

**Type of library, broken out by the total number of full-time equivalent employees at the participant's library or library system.**

| FTE Employees | Central library in a system | Entire library system | Branch library |
|---|---|---|---|
| Less than 10 | 42.86% | 28.57% | 28.57% |
| 10 to 49 | 15.38% | 38.46% | 46.15% |
| 50 or more | 100.00% | 0.00% | 0.00% |

**Total number of full-time equivalent employees at the participant's library or library system, broken out by type of library.**

| Type of Library | Less than 10 | 10 to 49 | 50 or more |
|---|---|---|---|
| Central library in a system | 33.33% | 22.22% | 44.44% |
| Entire library system | 28.57% | 71.43% | 0.00% |
| Branch library | 25.00% | 75.00% | 0.00% |

# SUMMARY OF MAIN FINDINGS

## CLASSES AT THE LIBRARY

### Job Search Skills

29.17 percent of all survey participants offer classes in the use of internet job boards. However, no branch libraries in the sample or any central or main libraries reported doing so, meaning that 53.85 percent of all participants reporting for an entire library system offer these types of classes. As library size grows, so too does the likelihood of offering classes on the use of internet job boards: whereas 22.22 percent of those libraries with less than 10 FTE employees offer these classes, this figure rises to 28.57 percent for the next level (10 to 49 FTE employees), and then all the way up to 37.5 percent for those libraries with 50 or more FTE employees.

Exactly half of all survey participants offer classes in general job search skills, including 69.23 percent of those participants reporting for an entire library systems. While no branch libraries in the sample offer such classes, 42.86 percent of central libraries do. As with before, the larger the library the more likely they are to offer a class on this subject, from just 33.33 percent of those with less than 10 employees ballooning up to 75 percent of those with 50 or more employees.

Just less than half (45.83 percent) of all libraries in the sample offer classes in resume writing. This is more popular with entire library systems (53.85 percent) and branch libraries (50 percent) than it is with central or main libraries (28.57 percent). Broken out by FTE library employees, the smallest libraries (less than 10 employees) and the largest libraries (50 or more employees) offer resume writing classes most often, at 55.56 and 50 percent, respectively, while just 28.57 percent of those libraries with 10 to 49 employees offer such a class.

### Exam Prep and ESL

Just 20.83 percent of libraries in the sample offer GED or other high school equivalency classes. No participating central libraries reported doing this, while 30.77 percent of all participants reporting for an entire library system said they offer such a class, as did 25 percent of the branch libraries in the sample. Broken out by FTE employees, those libraries with 50 or more employees offer these types of classes 37.5 percent of the time, while all other libraries do so between 10 and 15 percent.

Even fewer libraries offer classes in civil service exam preparation. In fact, just 8.33 percent of all libraries in the sample offer these types of classes. No central or main libraries have them, nor do any libraries with 10 to 49 FTE employees. While 25 percent of branch libraries offer civil service exam prep (1 in 4), only 7.69 percent of those participants reporting for an entire library system do the same.

The numbers for ESL (English as a Second Language) classes are similar: only 12.5 percent of all survey participants offer these classes. Again, no classes are offered at central/main libraries or at any libraries in the 10 to 49 FTE employees range, and again 25 percent (1 in 4) of branch libraries in the sample do. There is a slight increase in those libraries with 50 or more FTE employees, up to 25 percent here, as there is a similar increase for those participants reporting for an entire library system, up to 15.38 percent.

### Social Networks

We asked survey participants if the library offers classes in the use of any of the following social networks for job search purposes: Facebook; LinkedIn; and YouTube. Facebook proved to be the favorite, with 25 percent of all participants saying they offer such courses in the use of the social network, with LinkedIn coming in a close second at 20.38 percent. While no branch libraries in the sample offer classes in the use of Facebook, 28.57 percent of main/central libraries do, as do 30.77 percent of those participants reporting for an entire library system. The largest libraries (with 50 or more FTE employees) have these classes 37.5 percent of the time, while just 14.29 percent of those libraries with 10 to 49 employees can say the same. As for classes in the use of LinkedIn, branch libraries again do not offer these classes, while 30.77 percent of those participants reporting for an entire library system do. Once again, the largest libraries are more likely to offer such classes, as 37.5 percent of those libraries in the sample with 50 or more employees do, the highest percentage in its category.

Only one library in the sample offers classes in the use of YouTube for job search purposes. This participant is reporting for an entire library system with less than 10 FTE employees.

## RESOURCES AND OTHER INSTRUCTIONAL MATERIALS

### Spending on Materials

In the past year, the libraries in the sample spent a mean of $15,498 on books, CDs, instructional materials, eBooks, databases, and other materials specifically for addressing or equipping the job center with reference and educational materials, or approximately $2,661 per FTE employee. While 8 participants spent a total of $500 or less in this respect, there were 5 participants that spent at least $10,000, with one participant spending as much as $150,000. The overall median was $1,250, or $177 per employee. Branch libraries spent just a mean of $300 (and a maximum of only $500), while central libraries posted a mean of $13,686 and those reporting for entire library systems posted a mean of $21,327. The mean spending for those libraries with 50 or more FTE employees was $30,263, although this was influenced greatly by the one response of $150,000 as the median here was just $300. Per employee, the smallest libraries (with less than 10 employees) spent the most, a mean of $6,055.

### Advertisements of Job Availabilities

34.78 percent of survey participants say their library serves as a conduit for want ads or other advertisements of job availabilities either through a bulletin board, listserv, or some other information device. Whereas just 14.29 percent of central libraries perform this function, 50 percent of all those participants reporting for an entire library system say their library does just that. For those with 50 or more employees, the figure is above the average at 42.86 percent, while those with 10 to 49 employees are well below that mark at 28.57 percent.

No libraries in the sample have prepared a video or podcast on how to use the library's overall job-finding resources.

## THE JOB CENTER SPACE

### Visitors

The employment information centers (or similar reference collections) at the libraries in the sample each attract a mean of 54.23 visitors per week. The median here is 32.5, and the range is from 2.5 to 200 weekly visitors. Branch libraries report a mean of only 20 such visitors, while central libraries attract a mean of 46.79 and those reporting for an entire library system a mean of 67.13. Broken out by FTE employees, those libraries in the middle range (10 to 49 employees) posted the highest mean (72.14) and median (100). By comparison, the next closest mean and median both belong to the "50 or more employees" range at 50.43 and 50, respectively.

The libraries in the sample report a mean increase of 14.28 percent in such visitors over the past three years. The median is 10 percent and the maximum is 80 percent. While one library cites its number of visitors to the job center has decreased by 50 percent over this time, this proved to be one of only three participants in the sample that claimed a decrease, with the other two citing decreases of just 4 and 5 percent. As the number of FTE employees at the library increases, this figure steadily decreases: while those libraries with less than 10 employees posted a mean increase of 19.38 percent, those in the "10 to 49" range had a mean of 13.2 percent while those with 50 or more employees posted a mean increase of just 7.2 percent.

### Job Fairs

18.18 percent of libraries in the sample have ever hosted a job fair, including 33.33 percent of central or main libraries and 37.5 percent of those libraries with less than 10 employees. On the other end of the spectrum, just 8.33 percent of those participants reporting for an entire library system say they have hosted a job fair, and no libraries in the "10 to 49" employees range have done so. 14.29 percent of libraries with 50 or more employees have held a job fair.

For those libraries in the sample that have hosted a job fair, the mean number of participants at such an event is 88.75. The median is actually higher than that at 92.5, and the range is from 30 to 140. Those job fairs held by libraries with 50 or more employees have the highest attendance numbers, with a mean of 120 participants, while those libraries with less than 10 employees attract a mean of 78.33 attendants at these job fairs. The mean for the participants reporting for an entire library system is 140, while the means for central libraries (75) and branch libraries (65) are both roughly half that figure.

## PARTNERSHIPS

### Churches and Other Houses of Worship

12.5 percent of survey participants say the library has partnered with churches or other houses of religious worship to sponsor classes in job search skills or to otherwise offer job search related advice and information. All of these participants were reporting for an entire library system, and all had at least 10 employees. 28.57 percent of those libraries in the "10 to 49" employees range say they have partnered with such institutions.

### Other Non-Profit Organizations and Unions

14 of 24 survey participants (58.33 percent) have partnered with other non-profit organizations to sponsor job search classes or to offer related advice and information. These partnerships are most popular among those participants reporting for an entire library system (69.23 percent), while 50 percent of branch libraries and 42.86 percent of central libraries have established such partnerships. 44.44 percent of those libraries with less than 10 FTE employees have partnered with other non-profit organizations for these purposes, the lowest percentage in this category, while 71.43 percent of those libraries with 10 to 49 FTE employees and 62.5 percent of those with 50 or more employees have done so.

No library in the sample has partnered with a union for purposes of job search classes or related information.

### K-12 Schools and Colleges

29.17 percent of libraries in the sample have partnered with K-12 schools to sponsor job search classes. The splits among the different types of libraries are fairly even, ranging between 25 percent and 30.77 percent. When the data is broken out by the number of FTE employees, however, the range is much broader, from a low of 14.29 percent for those libraries with 10 to 49 employees to a high of 50 percent of those libraries with 50 or more employees.

Not as many libraries partner with colleges for these purposes, as just 12.5 percent of survey participants reported doing so. No branch libraries in the sample have established such partnerships, nor have any libraries with 10 to 49 employees. Whereas 11.11 percent of the smallest libraries (those with less than 10 employees) have partnered with colleges for job search purposes, 25 percent of those libraries with 50 or more employees have established such relationships.

### Government Agencies

Exactly half of all survey participants have partnered with government agencies for job search purposes. While just 28.57 percent of central libraries in the sample have done so, 50 percent of all branch libraries and 61.54 percent of participants reporting for an entire library system have partnered with such agencies. Broken out by number of FTE library employees, those libraries in the middle range (10 to 49) have partnered with government agencies most often at 57.14 percent, while the smallest libraries in the sample (less than 10 employees) have done so just 44.44 percent of the time.

### Career Coaches

Only one survey participant (4.17 percent of the sample) employs or contracts a career coach at the library to help patrons. This participant was reporting for an entire library system with 50 or more employees. The majority of libraries in the sample (62.5 percent) "don't really get involved in this," while the remaining 33.33 percent will put patrons in touch with a career coach or give them a list of coaches. Central libraries are the least active in this respect, with 71.43 percent of them reporting that they don't get involved with career coaches. Compare this to 61.54 percent for entire library systems and 50 percent for the branch libraries in the sample. Broken out by number of FTE employees at the library, those libraries in the "10 to 49" employees range are unlikely to hire a career coach, as 85.71 percent do not get involved, while 44.44 percent of those with less than 10 employees and 37.5 percent of those with 50 or more employees will put patrons in touch with a coach or give patrons a list of coaches.

## LIBRARY STAFF

### Staff Time Devoted to Job Searches

The libraries in the sample estimate an average of 14.95 percent of the library staff's time is dedicated to assisting job seekers. The median here is 10 percent, while the range is from a low of 2 percent to a high of 50 percent. Branch libraries have the lowest mean at 8.33 percent and in fact no branch library responded higher than 10 percent. The mean for those participants reporting for an entire library system is 18.18 percent. Broken out by FTE employees, the libraries with 10 to 49 employees have the highest mean at 18.86 percent, although this is aided by one respondent's answer of 50 percent; these libraries in fact have the lowest median at 5 percent. Those libraries with 50 or more employees compiled a mean of 13.67 percent and a median of 12.5 percent, while those libraries with less than 10 employees had a mean of 12.14 percent and a median of 10 percent.

### Job Center Personnel

18.18 percent of survey participants say their library has one or more persons specifically devoted to the job center or to job center related activities, including 25 percent of those participants reporting for an entire library system. No branch libraries in the sample have such a person. As library size increases, so too does the likelihood of the library having a person on staff specifically devoted to the job center: 12.5 percent of libraries with less than 10 employees have such a person, and this figure rises slightly to 14.29 percent for the "10 to 49" employees range before doubling to 28.57 percent for those libraries with 50 or more employees.

## ONLINE PRESENCE

We asked survey participants if the library's job center maintains an online presence on a number of different venues that discusses and presents the job center's resources.

### Library Website

45.83 percent of survey participants say the library's job center has an online presence on the library's website. This is less likely for central libraries, as just 28.57 percent of them maintain such a presence on the library website. 53.85 percent of participants reporting for an entire library system say the library has such a presence. The bigger the library, the more likely it is for the job center to have a presence on the library's website: 33.33 percent of libraries with less than 10 FTE employees say this is the case, a figure which rises to 42.86 percent for the "10 to 49" employees range and then all the way up to 62.5 percent for those libraries with 50 or more employees.

### Local Government Website

Just two participants (8.33 percent of the sample) say the library's job center has a presence on the local government's website. These are both participants reporting for an entire library system, one with less than 10 FTE employees and the other with 50 or more employees.

### Library's LinkedIn and Facebook Pages

Just two participants say the library's job center has a presence on the library's LinkedIn page, with both participants reporting for an entire library system, and both have 50 or more employees. Likewise, just two participants say the job center has a presence on the library's Facebook page. Both of these participants are reporting for an entire library system, one with less than 10 employees and the other with 50 or more employees.

### Library's Google+ and YouTube Pages

No survey participants say their library's job center has a presence on the library's Google+ page or the library's YouTube page.

# 1. Classes at the Library

**Table 1.1: Does the library offer classes in the use of internet job boards?**

| | Yes | No |
|---|---|---|
| Entire sample | 29.17% | 70.83% |

**Table 1.2: Does the library offer classes in the use of internet job boards? Broken out by type of library.**

| Type of Library | Yes | No |
|---|---|---|
| Central library in a system | 0.00% | 100.00% |
| Entire library system | 53.85% | 46.15% |
| Branch library | 0.00% | 100.00% |

**Table 1.3: Does the library offer classes in the use of internet job boards? Broken out by the total number of full-time equivalent employees at the participant's library or library system.**

| FTE Employees | Yes | No |
|---|---|---|
| Less than 10 | 22.22% | 77.78% |
| 10 to 49 | 28.57% | 71.43% |
| 50 or more | 37.50% | 62.50% |

**Table 1.4: Does the library offer classes in general job search skills?**

| | Yes | No |
|---|---|---|
| Entire sample | 50.00% | 50.00% |

**Table 1.5: Does the library offer classes in general job search skills? Broken out by type of library.**

| Type of Library | Yes | No |
|---|---|---|
| Central library in a system | 42.86% | 57.14% |
| Entire library system | 69.23% | 30.77% |
| Branch library | 0.00% | 100.00% |

**Table 1.6: Does the library offer classes in general job search skills? Broken out by the total number of full-time equivalent employees at the participant's library or library system.**

| FTE Employees | Yes | No |
|---|---|---|
| Less than 10 | 33.33% | 66.67% |
| 10 to 49 | 42.86% | 57.14% |
| 50 or more | 75.00% | 25.00% |

**Table 1.7: Does the library offer classes in resume writing?**

| | Yes | No |
|---|---|---|
| Entire sample | 45.83% | 54.17% |

**Table 1.8: Does the library offer classes in resume writing? Broken out by type of library.**

| Type of Library | Yes | No |
|---|---|---|
| Central library in a system | 28.57% | 71.43% |
| Entire library system | 53.85% | 46.15% |
| Branch library | 50.00% | 50.00% |

**Table 1.9: Does the library offer classes in resume writing? Broken out by the total number of full-time equivalent employees at the participant's library or library system.**

| FTE Employees | Yes | No |
|---|---|---|
| Less than 10 | 55.56% | 44.44% |
| 10 to 49 | 28.57% | 71.43% |
| 50 or more | 50.00% | 50.00% |

**Table 1.10: Does the library offer GED or other high school equivalency classes?**

| | Yes | No |
|---|---|---|
| Entire sample | 20.83% | 79.17% |

**Table 1.11: Does the library offer GED or other high school equivalency classes? Broken out by type of library.**

| Type of Library | Yes | No |
|---|---|---|
| Central library in a system | 0.00% | 100.00% |
| Entire library system | 30.77% | 69.23% |
| Branch library | 25.00% | 75.00% |

**Table 1.12: Does the library offer GED or other high school equivalency classes? Broken out by the total number of full-time equivalent employees at the participant's library or library system.**

| FTE Employees | Yes | No |
|---|---|---|
| Less than 10 | 11.11% | 88.89% |
| 10 to 49 | 14.29% | 85.71% |
| 50 or more | 37.50% | 62.50% |

**Table 1.13: Does the library offer classes in civil service exam preparation?**

| | Yes | No |
|---|---|---|
| Entire sample | 8.33% | 91.67% |

**Table 1.14: Does the library offer classes in civil service exam preparation? Broken out by type of library.**

| Type of Library | Yes | No |
|---|---|---|
| Central library in a system | 0.00% | 100.00% |
| Entire library system | 7.69% | 92.31% |
| Branch library | 25.00% | 75.00% |

**Table 1.15: Does the library offer classes in civil service exam preparation? Broken out by the total number of full-time equivalent employees at the participant's library or library system.**

| FTE Employees | Yes | No |
|---|---|---|
| Less than 10 | 11.11% | 88.89% |
| 10 to 49 | 0.00% | 100.00% |
| 50 or more | 12.50% | 87.50% |

**Table 1.16: Does the library offer ESL (English as a Second Language) classes?**

| | Yes | No |
|---|---|---|
| Entire sample | 12.50% | 87.50% |

**Table 1.17: Does the library offer ESL (English as a Second Language) classes? Broken out by type of library.**

| Type of Library | Yes | No |
|---|---|---|
| Central library in a system | 0.00% | 100.00% |
| Entire library system | 15.38% | 84.62% |
| Branch library | 25.00% | 75.00% |

**Table 1.18: Does the library offer ESL (English as a Second Language) classes? Broken out by the total number of full-time equivalent employees at the participant's library or library system.**

| FTE Employees | Yes | No |
|---|---|---|
| Less than 10 | 11.11% | 88.89% |
| 10 to 49 | 0.00% | 100.00% |
| 50 or more | 25.00% | 75.00% |

**Table 1.19: Does the library offer classes in the use of Facebook for job search purposes (or cover its use in general classes about job searches)?**

| | Yes | No |
|---|---|---|
| Entire sample | 25.00% | 75.00% |

**Table 1.20: Does the library offer classes in the use of Facebook for job search purposes (or cover its use in general classes about job searches)? Broken out by type of library.**

| Type of Library | Yes | No |
|---|---|---|
| Central library in a system | 28.57% | 71.43% |
| Entire library system | 30.77% | 69.23% |
| Branch library | 0.00% | 100.00% |

**Table 1.21: Does the library offer classes in the use of Facebook for job search purposes (or cover its use in general classes about job searches)? Broken out by the total number of full-time equivalent employees at the participant's library or library system.**

| FTE Employees | Yes | No |
|---|---|---|
| Less than 10 | 22.22% | 77.78% |
| 10 to 49 | 14.29% | 85.71% |
| 50 or more | 37.50% | 62.50% |

**Table 1.22: Does the library offer classes in the use of LinkedIn for job search purposes (or cover its use in general classes about job searches)?**

| | Yes | No |
|---|---|---|
| Entire sample | 20.83% | 79.17% |

**Table 1.23: Does the library offer classes in the use of LinkedIn for job search purposes (or cover its use in general classes about job searches)? Broken out by type of library.**

| Type of Library | Yes | No |
|---|---|---|
| Central library in a system | 14.29% | 85.71% |
| Entire library system | 30.77% | 69.23% |
| Branch library | 0.00% | 100.00% |

**Table 1.24: Does the library offer classes in the use of LinkedIn for job search purposes (or cover its use in general classes about job searches)? Broken out by the total number of full-time equivalent employees at the participant's library or library system.**

| FTE Employees | Yes | No |
|---|---|---|
| Less than 10 | 11.11% | 88.89% |
| 10 to 49 | 14.29% | 85.71% |
| 50 or more | 37.50% | 62.50% |

**Table 1.25: Does the library offer classes in the use of YouTube for job search purposes (or cover its use in general classes about job searches)?**

| | Yes | No |
|---|---|---|
| Entire sample | 4.17% | 95.83% |

**Table 1.26: Does the library offer classes in the use of YouTube for job search purposes (or cover its use in general classes about job searches)? Broken out by type of library.**

| Type of Library | Yes | No |
|---|---|---|
| Central library in a system | 0.00% | 100.00% |
| Entire library system | 7.69% | 92.31% |
| Branch library | 0.00% | 100.00% |

**Table 1.27: Does the library offer classes in the use of YouTube for job search purposes (or cover its use in general classes about job searches)? Broken out by the total number of full-time equivalent employees at the participant's library or library system.**

| FTE Employees | Yes | No |
|---|---|---|
| Less than 10 | 11.11% | 88.89% |
| 10 to 49 | 0.00% | 100.00% |
| 50 or more | 0.00% | 100.00% |

# 2. Resources and Other Instructional Materials

**Table 2.1: In the past year, how much did the library spend on books, CDs, instructional materials, eBooks, databases, and other materials specifically to address or equip the job center with reference and educational materials?**

| | Mean | Median | Minimum | Maximum |
|---|---|---|---|---|
| Entire sample | $15,498.25 | $1,250.00 | $0.00 | $150,000.00 |

**Table 2.2: In the past year, how much did the library spend on books, CDs, instructional materials, eBooks, databases, and other materials specifically to address or equip the job center with reference and educational materials? Broken out by type of library.**

| Type of Library | Mean | Median | Minimum | Maximum |
|---|---|---|---|---|
| Central library in a system | $13,685.71 | $1,500.00 | $0.00 | $80,000.00 |
| Entire library system | $21,326.50 | $3,000.00 | $15.00 | $150,000.00 |
| Branch library | $300.00 | $200.00 | $200.00 | $500.00 |

**Table 2.3: In the past year, how much did the library spend on books, CDs, instructional materials, eBooks, databases, and other materials specifically to address or equip the job center with reference and educational materials? Broken out by the total number of full-time equivalent employees at the participant's library or library system.**

| FTE Employees | Mean | Median | Minimum | Maximum |
|---|---|---|---|---|
| Less than 10 | $13,925.00 | $1,250.00 | $200.00 | $80,000.00 |
| 10 to 49 | $6,750.00 | $5,000.00 | $250.00 | $20,500.00 |
| 50 or more | $30,263.00 | $300.00 | $0.00 | $150,000.00 |

**Table 2.4: In the past year, how much did the library spend on books, CDs, instructional materials, eBooks, databases, and other materials specifically to address or equip the job center with reference and educational materials? Per full-time equivalent employee.**

| | Mean | Median | Minimum | Maximum | Index |
|---|---|---|---|---|---|
| Entire sample | $2,661.47 | $177.08 | $0.00 | $40,000.00 | 100.0 |

**Table 2.5: In the past year, how much did the library spend on books, CDs, instructional materials, eBooks, databases, and other materials specifically to address or equip the job center with reference and educational materials? Per full-time equivalent employee, broken out by type of library.**

| Type of Library | Mean | Median | Minimum | Maximum | Index |
|---|---|---|---|---|---|
| Central library in a system | $6,040.41 | $277.78 | $0.00 | $40,000.00 | 227.0 |
| Entire library system | $1,079.82 | $218.75 | $0.04 | $6,250.00 | 40.6 |
| Branch library | $49.44 | $40.00 | $25.00 | $83.33 | 1.9 |

**Table 2.6: In the past year, how much did the library spend on books, CDs, instructional materials, eBooks, databases, and other materials specifically to address or equip the job center with reference and educational materials? Per full-time equivalent employee, broken out by the total number of full-time equivalent employees at the participant's library or library system.**

| FTE Employees | Mean | Median | Minimum | Maximum | Index |
|---|---|---|---|---|---|
| Less than 10 | $6,055.00 | $270.83 | $25.00 | $40,000.00 | 227.5 |
| 10 to 49 | $252.65 | $250.00 | $13.89 | $683.33 | 9.5 |
| 50 or more | $604.17 | $5.08 | $0.00 | $3,000.00 | 22.7 |

**Name some of the most heavily used resources in your job information center or job related reference collection.**

1. Computers, TN jobs website, our online career center at wcpltn.org, fliers from local agencies.
2. Jobs/test databases and test books.
3. Job & Career Accelerator from Learning Express.
4. Meetings with career coach; resume books.
5. Resume writing material.
6. Resume builder.
7. NOVEL databases, Indeed.com, Civil Service Practice Tests.
8. JobNow database; Occupational Outlook; resume, cover letter, interview books.
9. In our small branch library, patrons tend to mostly use internet-based resources available via our library system website.
10. Resume and cover letter writing books.
11. Internet access and one-on-one assistance from library staff; resume and interview books.
12. RefUSA, LexisNexis, Business Insights databases.
13. We don't have a collection, just a lab.
14. Career Builder Web search. Learn A Test Web site.
15. Reference USA, Fergusons Testing & Education Center; Facts on File Career Center.
16. Computers with internet, resume software & related books.
17. Resume writing skills.
18. Databases.
19. Resume books.
20. ohiomeansjobs.com; LearningExpress Library, WinWay Resume Software, MIcrosoft Word Resume/Cover Letter templates.
21. Local newspaper classified ads.

**Table 2.7: Does the library itself serve as a conduit for want ads or other advertisements of job availabilities either through a bulletin board, listserv, or other information device?**

| | Yes | No |
|---|---|---|
| Entire sample | 34.78% | 65.22% |

**Table 2.8: Does the library itself serve as a conduit for want ads or other advertisements of job availabilities either through a bulletin board, listserv, or other information device? Broken out by type of library.**

| Type of Library | Yes | No |
|---|---|---|
| Central library in a system | 14.29% | 85.71% |
| Entire library system | 50.00% | 50.00% |
| Branch library | 25.00% | 75.00% |

**Table 2.9: Does the library itself serve as a conduit for want ads or other advertisements of job availabilities either through a bulletin board, listserv, or other information device? Broken out by the total number of full-time equivalent employees at the participant's library or library system.**

| FTE Employees | Yes | No |
|---|---|---|
| Less than 10 | 33.33% | 66.67% |
| 10 to 49 | 28.57% | 71.43% |
| 50 or more | 42.86% | 57.14% |

**Table 2.10: Has the library itself prepared a video or podcast on how to use the library's overall job-finding resources?**

| | Yes | No |
|---|---|---|
| Entire sample | 0.00% | 100.00% |

**What materials or resources are you planning to purchase in the near future to enhance your job research information center or collection and why are you going to purchase such resources?**

1. Due to fiscal constraints, we are working to maintain currency in book collection and updating the online career center.

2. Another database from Gale.

3. Assessments for seminar use; DVDs about occupational information and new edition career related books.

4. Limited budget, so will depend on what will be available in 2013.

5. Our materials are purchased through a central collection development department that serves our library system as a whole.

6. With our recent "Libraries for Job Seekers" Grant, we totally overhauled our job seekers collection. We are now only buying new titles or updated versions of current titles to keep the collection updated.

7. In general, more/newer print materials. Our patrons have access to online assistance through a state-wide job assistance site. Many people are not comfortable with that, and prefer working with print.

8. Continue use of databases.

9. We are not purchasing for this lab; we may not even be able to fund the nonprofit worker next year, so it may go away altogether.

10. Will be upgrading our operating systems on all computers; adding ram to computers to install virtual Lynix.

11. Yes - more books and career related books to meet the need and stay current with changes in the job market.

12. Moe resume writing materials to keep up with demand.

13. There is no change at the moment.

14. Resume books... more, more, and more are needed.

# 3. The Job Center Space

**Table 3.1: How many visitors does the library's employment information center or reference collection attract in a typical week?**

| | Mean | Median | Minimum | Maximum |
|---|---|---|---|---|
| Entire sample | 54.23 | 32.50 | 2.50 | 200.00 |

**Table 3.2: How many visitors does the library's employment information center or reference collection attract in a typical week? Broken out by type of library.**

| Type of Library | Mean | Median | Minimum | Maximum |
|---|---|---|---|---|
| Central library in a system | 46.79 | 35.00 | 2.50 | 125.00 |
| Entire library system | 67.13 | 55.00 | 2.50 | 200.00 |
| Branch library | 20.00 | 20.00 | 10.00 | 30.00 |

**Table 3.3: How many visitors does the library's employment information center or reference collection attract in a typical week? Broken out by the total number of full-time equivalent employees at the participant's library or library system.**

| FTE Employees | Mean | Median | Minimum | Maximum |
|---|---|---|---|---|
| Less than 10 | 41.88 | 17.50 | 10.00 | 200.00 |
| 10 to 49 | 72.14 | 100.00 | 2.50 | 150.00 |
| 50 or more | 50.43 | 50.00 | 3.00 | 100.00 |

**Table 3.4: What has been the average annual percentage increase (or decrease) in such visitors over the past three years?**

| | Mean | Median | Minimum | Maximum |
|---|---|---|---|---|
| **Entire sample** | 14.28% | 10.00% | -50.00% | 80.00% |

**Table 3.5: What has been the average annual percentage increase (or decrease) in such visitors over the past three years? Broken out by type of library.**

| Type of Library | Mean | Median | Minimum | Maximum |
|---|---|---|---|---|
| **Central library in a system** | 13.20% | 10.00% | -5.00% | 35.00% |
| **Entire library system** | 16.10% | 12.50% | -50.00% | 80.00% |
| **Branch library** | 10.00% | 10.00% | 0.00% | 20.00% |

**Table 3.6: What has been the average annual percentage increase (or decrease) in such visitors over the past three years? Broken out by the total number of full-time equivalent employees at the participant's library or library system.**

| FTE Employees | Mean | Median | Minimum | Maximum |
|---|---|---|---|---|
| **Less than 10** | 19.38% | 20.00% | -5.00% | 50.00% |
| **10 to 49** | 13.20% | 10.00% | -50.00% | 80.00% |
| **50 or more** | 7.20% | 10.00% | 0.00% | 15.00% |

## How has the library adjusted its workstation access policies to accommodate those doing job-related research?

1. Our only concession has been to put a sign on our computer with a scanner so persons who need to actually use the scanner have access to it. Otherwise we have over 30 computers with generous time allowances.
2. We've opened two of our database computers to the internet to help patrons search for jobs.
3. There's several workstations that can only be accessed by people involved in the Career Transition Center.
4. Social network web sites are available for both patrons and our employees from any workstation, also from our public usage PCs. We have a social media policy for our employees.
5. Created workstations with a separation to provide privacy; also have a third computer at circ. desk if person needs more one-on-one assistance, especially if the reference staff is not available at the time.
6. We have a laptop that can be checked out for in-library use with no time limit up until closing time. We have two computers with two hour continuous internet service available by reservation.
7. Our regular public computer sessions are one hour, we regularly increase the allotted time for job searchers at their request.
8. People who are filling out applications or doing resumes may have as long as they need to complete the task.
9. Occasionally, we give the jobseeker more time on internet station if filling out a job application online.
10. The Worksource lab did not require a library card or limit time on the computer as long as the lab was open and the person was doing job related work.
11. Let people stay on computers for more than an hour for job applications and tests.
12. We do reserve computers specifically for employment workshops and one-on-one resume assistance. They can also tell a clerk if they are applying for a job or taking a test for a job, they can extend their time on the computer.
13. Anyone can and always has been able to access our PCS.
14. We stay open -- five nights a week till 9. Open all day Saturdays and Sunday afts all year long.
15. Lengthened access time per person per day.
16. Leaflets online access.
17. None, they have access to all job related searches.
18. We reserve certain computers strictly for job searchers or job related computing.

19. We have not - we are a community of approximately 27500 and we only have 8 public computers that access the internet spread into 3 different parts of our library building. We don't have a large enough building to add more computers or to treat patrons with one need such as job seeking any differently than a patron with other needs such as using computers for research or entertainment.

**Table 3.7: Has the library ever held a job fair?**

| | Yes | No |
|---|---|---|
| Entire sample | 18.18% | 81.82% |

**Table 3.8: Has the library ever held a job fair? Broken out by type of library.**

| Type of Library | Yes | No |
|---|---|---|
| Central library in a system | 33.33% | 66.67% |
| Entire library system | 8.33% | 91.67% |
| Branch library | 25.00% | 75.00% |

**Table 3.9: Has the library ever held a job fair? Broken out by the total number of full-time equivalent employees at the participant's library or library system.**

| FTE Employees | Yes | No |
|---|---|---|
| Less than 10 | 37.50% | 62.50% |
| 10 to 49 | 0.00% | 100.00% |
| 50 or more | 14.29% | 85.71% |

**Table 3.10: If the library has ever held a job fair, how many participants attended?**

| | Mean | Median | Minimum | Maximum |
|---|---|---|---|---|
| Entire sample | 88.75 | 92.50 | 30.00 | 140.00 |

**Table 3.11: If the library has ever held a job fair, how many participants attended? Broken out by type of library.**

| Type of Library | Mean | Median | Minimum | Maximum |
|---|---|---|---|---|
| Central library in a system | 75.00 | 75.00 | 30.00 | 120.00 |
| Entire library system | 140.00 | 140.00 | 140.00 | 140.00 |
| Branch library | 65.00 | 65.00 | 65.00 | 65.00 |

**Table 3.12: If the library has ever held a job fair, how many participants attended? Broken out by the total number of full-time equivalent employees at the participant's library or library system.**

| FTE Employees | Mean | Median | Minimum | Maximum |
|---|---|---|---|---|
| Less than 10 | 78.33 | 65.00 | 30.00 | 140.00 |
| 10 to 49 | N/A | N/A | N/A | N/A |
| 50 or more | 120.00 | 120.00 | 120.00 | 120.00 |

# 4. Partnerships

**Table 4.1: Has the library partnered with churches or other houses of religious worship to sponsor classes in job search skills or to otherwise offer job search related advice and information?**

| | Yes | No |
|---|---|---|
| **Entire sample** | 12.50% | 87.50% |

**Table 4.2: Has the library partnered with churches or other houses of religious worship to sponsor classes in job search skills or to otherwise offer job search related advice and information? Broken out by type of library.**

| Type of Library | Yes | No |
|---|---|---|
| **Central library in a system** | 0.00% | 100.00% |
| **Entire library system** | 23.08% | 76.92% |
| **Branch library** | 0.00% | 100.00% |

**Table 4.3: Has the library partnered with churches or other houses of religious worship to sponsor classes in job search skills or to otherwise offer job search related advice and information? Broken out by the total number of full-time equivalent employees at the participant's library or library system.**

| FTE Employees | Yes | No |
|---|---|---|
| **Less than 10** | 0.00% | 100.00% |
| **10 to 49** | 28.57% | 71.43% |
| **50 or more** | 12.50% | 87.50% |

**Table 4.4: Has the library partnered with other non-profit organizations to sponsor classes in job search skills or to otherwise offer job search related advice and information?**

| | Yes | No |
|---|---|---|
| Entire sample | 58.33% | 41.67% |

**Table 4.5: Has the library partnered with other non-profit organizations to sponsor classes in job search skills or to otherwise offer job search related advice and information? Broken out by type of library.**

| Type of Library | Yes | No |
|---|---|---|
| Central library in a system | 42.86% | 57.14% |
| Entire library system | 69.23% | 30.77% |
| Branch library | 50.00% | 50.00% |

**Table 4.6: Has the library partnered with other non-profit organizations to sponsor classes in job search skills or to otherwise offer job search related advice and information? Broken out by the total number of full-time equivalent employees at the participant's library or library system.**

| FTE Employees | Yes | No |
|---|---|---|
| Less than 10 | 44.44% | 55.56% |
| 10 to 49 | 71.43% | 28.57% |
| 50 or more | 62.50% | 37.50% |

**Table 4.7: Has the library partnered with unions to sponsor classes in job search skills or to otherwise offer job search related advice and information?**

| | Yes | No |
|---|---|---|
| Entire sample | 0.00% | 100.00% |

**Table 4.8: Has the library partnered with K-12 schools to sponsor classes in job search skills or to otherwise offer job search related advice and information?**

| | Yes | No |
|---|---|---|
| Entire sample | 29.17% | 70.83% |

**Table 4.9: Has the library partnered with K-12 schools to sponsor classes in job search skills or to otherwise offer job search related advice and information? Broken out by type of library.**

| Type of Library | Yes | No |
|---|---|---|
| Central library in a system | 28.57% | 71.43% |
| Entire library system | 30.77% | 69.23% |
| Branch library | 25.00% | 75.00% |

**Table 4.10: Has the library partnered with K-12 schools to sponsor classes in job search skills or to otherwise offer job search related advice and information? Broken out by the total number of full-time equivalent employees at the participant's library or library system.**

| FTE Employees | Yes | No |
|---|---|---|
| Less than 10 | 22.22% | 77.78% |
| 10 to 49 | 14.29% | 85.71% |
| 50 or more | 50.00% | 50.00% |

**Table 4.11: Has the library partnered with colleges to sponsor classes in job search skills or to otherwise offer job search related advice and information?**

| | Yes | No |
|---|---|---|
| **Entire sample** | 12.50% | 87.50% |

**Table 4.12: Has the library partnered with colleges to sponsor classes in job search skills or to otherwise offer job search related advice and information? Broken out by type of library.**

| Type of Library | Yes | No |
|---|---|---|
| **Central library in a system** | 14.29% | 85.71% |
| **Entire library system** | 15.38% | 84.62% |
| **Branch library** | 0.00% | 100.00% |

**Table 4.13: Has the library partnered with colleges to sponsor classes in job search skills or to otherwise offer job search related advice and information? Broken out by the total number of full-time equivalent employees at the participant's library or library system.**

| FTE Employees | Yes | No |
|---|---|---|
| **Less than 10** | 11.11% | 88.89% |
| **10 to 49** | 0.00% | 100.00% |
| **50 or more** | 25.00% | 75.00% |

**Table 4.14: Has the library partnered with government agencies to sponsor classes in job search skills or to otherwise offer job search related advice and information?**

| | Yes | No |
|---|---|---|
| Entire sample | 50.00% | 50.00% |

**Table 4.15: Has the library partnered with government agencies to sponsor classes in job search skills or to otherwise offer job search related advice and information? Broken out by type of library.**

| Type of Library | Yes | No |
|---|---|---|
| Central library in a system | 28.57% | 71.43% |
| Entire library system | 61.54% | 38.46% |
| Branch library | 50.00% | 50.00% |

**Table 4.16: Has the library partnered with government agencies to sponsor classes in job search skills or to otherwise offer job search related advice and information? Broken out by the total number of full-time equivalent employees at the participant's library or library system.**

| FTE Employees | Yes | No |
|---|---|---|
| Less than 10 | 44.44% | 55.56% |
| 10 to 49 | 57.14% | 42.86% |
| 50 or more | 50.00% | 50.00% |

**If you have had cooperative relationships with other organizations in developing or supplying job search information or skills, please briefly describe these ventures.**

1. We post information from Goodwill Career Center and WorkForce Essentials Career center. Investigating the possibility of WFECC offering classes at the library. They have hosted at least 2 job fairs in our meeting room with large attendance numbers.
2. At first these people came to us. It was such a good partnership that we branched out and fostered more partnerships to market what we have/can do for our patrons and community.
3. We have conducted classes at the organizations' locations and shared speakers. we have hosted other organization's functions.
4. We opened a career transition centers that we've devoted space to. Independent people staff it and hold programs, consultations, etc.
5. One of our state-government sponsored workforce centers is located in one of our library buildings.
6. Years ago we partnered with a local college but that hasn't been in effect for a few years.
7. We received funding and programming assistance from two for profit businesses for our "Libraries for Jobseekers" grant.
8. Worked with the local Job Center to supply internet access when their hours were cut.
9. Goodwill.
10. They supply the personnel, materials and training; we just supply the computer lab.
11. Worked with State Farm for resume assistance and other job search classes. Worked with United Way for job-related classes.
12. Providing space for a jobs night where employers meet with possible applicants.
13. Work with local literacy nonprofit to provide job-search skills in computer lab.
14. We are currently in the process of partnering with Work Force Services, but we are in the beginning stages.
15. The School Corporation operates GED classes in library space.
16. Giving some look on fields in a special library.
17. Jobs and Family Services donated 8 computers to our library reserved for job searching, resumes, and any job related computing. We teach free computer classes on job search skills and work-related/basic computer skills. Our county's Jobs and Family Services promotes these services to its clientele as well as the general public.
18. We work with the local high school and the local job service from time to time to help students in transition to work programs such as WIA and other locally initiated programs through the school district.

**Table 4.17: Which phrase best describes the library's attitude toward the use of career coaches?**

| | We employ or contract one or more at the library to help patrons | We will put patrons in touch with a career coach or give them a list of coaches | We don't really get involved in this at this point |
|---|---|---|---|
| Entire sample | 4.17% | 33.33% | 62.50% |

**Table 4.18: Which phrase best describes the library's attitude toward the use of career coaches? Broken out by type of library.**

| Type of Library | We employ or contract one or more at the library to help patrons | We will put patrons in touch with a career coach or give them a list of coaches | We don't really get involved in this at this point |
|---|---|---|---|
| Central library in a system | 0.00% | 28.57% | 71.43% |
| Entire library system | 7.69% | 30.77% | 61.54% |
| Branch library | 0.00% | 50.00% | 50.00% |

**Table 4.19: Which phrase best describes the library's attitude toward the use of career coaches? Broken out by the total number of full-time equivalent employees at the participant's library or library system.**

| FTE Employees | We employ or contract one or more at the library to help patrons | We will put patrons in touch with a career coach or give them a list of coaches | We don't really get involved in this at this point |
|---|---|---|---|
| Less than 10 | 0.00% | 44.44% | 55.56% |
| 10 to 49 | 0.00% | 14.29% | 85.71% |
| 50 or more | 12.50% | 37.50% | 50.00% |

# 5. Library Staff

**Table 5.1: About what percentage of reference library staff time would you say is taken up by assistance to job seekers?**

| | Mean | Median | Minimum | Maximum |
|---|---|---|---|---|
| Entire sample | 14.95% | 10.00% | 2.00% | 50.00% |

**Table 5.2: About what percentage of reference library staff time would you say is taken up by assistance to job seekers? Broken out by type of library.**

| Type of Library | Mean | Median | Minimum | Maximum |
|---|---|---|---|---|
| Central library in a system | 12.33% | 12.50% | 2.00% | 25.00% |
| Entire library system | 18.18% | 10.00% | 5.00% | 50.00% |
| Branch library | 8.33% | 10.00% | 5.00% | 10.00% |

**Table 5.3: About what percentage of reference library staff time would you say is taken up by assistance to job seekers? Broken out by the total number of full-time equivalent employees at the participant's library or library system.**

| FTE Employees | Mean | Median | Minimum | Maximum |
|---|---|---|---|---|
| Less than 10 | 12.14% | 10.00% | 5.00% | 20.00% |
| 10 to 49 | 18.86% | 5.00% | 2.00% | 50.00% |
| 50 or more | 13.67% | 12.50% | 2.00% | 25.00% |

**Table 5.4: Does the library have one or more persons specifically devoted to a job center or job center related activities?**

| | Yes | No |
|---|---|---|
| **Entire sample** | 18.18% | 81.82% |

**Table 5.5: Does the library have one or more persons specifically devoted to a job center or job center related activities? Broken out by type of library.**

| Type of Library | Yes | No |
|---|---|---|
| **Central library in a system** | 16.67% | 83.33% |
| **Entire library system** | 25.00% | 75.00% |
| **Branch library** | 0.00% | 100.00% |

**Table 5.6: Does the library have one or more persons specifically devoted to a job center or job center related activities? Broken out by the total number of full-time equivalent employees at the participant's library or library system.**

| FTE Employees | Yes | No |
|---|---|---|
| **Less than 10** | 12.50% | 87.50% |
| **10 to 49** | 14.29% | 85.71% |
| **50 or more** | 28.57% | 71.43% |

**Explain your personnel strategy for your jobs research effort. Do you have one or more specialists? Do you hire freelancers or contractors to teach classes in resume writing, internet job board use, interviewing skills, and other areas? What is your strategy and how do you deploy staff and other labor?**

1. This is just one of our Reference Department responsibilities. We will review a person's resume for spelling & format errors. All we ask is for them to schedule an appointment although we do do it on the fly. It isn't generally asked for though.

2. We are so short-staffed and small that we cannot afford a dedicated person for this. instead we have trained all staff on basic jobs info/what we have to offer so they can all market our materials/dbs - and then patrons come downstairs to the ref area for help.

3. Direct people to the Job & Career Accelerator from LearningExpress.

4. One half-time dedicated career coach on staff.

5. Separate Career Transition staff, plus we do monthly computer programs w/ our own staff.

6. Some of our staff members and volunteers provide general PC/Internet training. This invariably involves some help with using online job boards and submitting job applications online. We also have 2 full-time literacy specialists who help patrons with ESL and GED prep. Most other job research efforts are handled by the workforce center located in one of our library branches and guest speakers, freelancers and contractors.

7. We are a very small library and do referrals as necessary to other larger libraries or the local Job Source organization.

8. Our reference librarian and director provide the day to day assistance. We have had special programs where we have hired certified resume reviewers, research specialists and others to teach workshops. We have also had a great response from members of the community offering free workshops in their area of expertise.

9. We are a very small library with no room to offer classes, no qualified staff to teach them, and no money to hire specialists. We do what we can to help job-seekers one-on-one.

10. Two librarians devote their time to this.

11. We hire a part-time nonprofit agency to staff our lab. He works with patrons on all of the above job skills.

12. We have local people do seminars that are career coaches.

13. We don't hire freelancers or contractors, but we do have two volunteer specialists that help with classes for job searching. We are not currently looking to use staff time for this endeavor, but we will help patrons if there is a need. We do want to continue to offer classes on job searching as demanded and we are able.

14. We hire freelancers to teach resume prep, internet job board use, interview skills.

15. No money for strategy. We rely on our librarians.

16. Our reference librarians teach classes as well as help with computer searches.

17. We have no strategy.

# 6. Online Presence

**Table 6.1: Does the library job center have an online presence on the library's website that discusses and presents the job center's resources?**

| | Yes | No |
|---|---|---|
| Entire sample | 45.83% | 54.17% |

**Table 6.2: Does the library job center have an online presence on the library's website that discusses and presents the job center's resources? Broken out by type of library.**

| Type of Library | Yes | No |
|---|---|---|
| Central library in a system | 28.57% | 71.43% |
| Entire library system | 53.85% | 46.15% |
| Branch library | 50.00% | 50.00% |

**Table 6.3: Does the library job center have an online presence on the library's website that discusses and presents the job center's resources? Broken out by the total number of full-time equivalent employees at the participant's library or library system.**

| FTE Employees | Yes | No |
|---|---|---|
| Less than 10 | 33.33% | 66.67% |
| 10 to 49 | 42.86% | 57.14% |
| 50 or more | 62.50% | 37.50% |

**Table 6.4: Does the library job center have an online presence on the local government's website that discusses and presents the job center's resources?**

| | Yes | No |
|---|---|---|
| Entire sample | 8.33% | 91.67% |

**Table 6.5: Does the library job center have an online presence on the local government's website that discusses and presents the job center's resources? Broken out by type of library.**

| Type of Library | Yes | No |
|---|---|---|
| Central library in a system | 0.00% | 100.00% |
| Entire library system | 15.38% | 84.62% |
| Branch library | 0.00% | 100.00% |

**Table 6.6: Does the library job center have an online presence on the local government's website that discusses and presents the job center's resources? Broken out by the total number of full-time equivalent employees at the participant's library or library system.**

| FTE Employees | Yes | No |
|---|---|---|
| Less than 10 | 11.11% | 88.89% |
| 10 to 49 | 0.00% | 100.00% |
| 50 or more | 12.50% | 87.50% |

**Table 6.7: Does the library job center have an online presence on the library's LinkedIn page that discusses and presents the job center's resources?**

| | Yes | No |
|---|---|---|
| Entire sample | 8.33% | 91.67% |

**Table 6.8: Does the library job center have an online presence on the library's LinkedIn page that discusses and presents the job center's resources? Broken out by type of library.**

| Type of Library | Yes | No |
|---|---|---|
| Central library in a system | 0.00% | 100.00% |
| Entire library system | 15.38% | 84.62% |
| Branch library | 0.00% | 100.00% |

**Table 6.9: Does the library job center have an online presence on the library's LinkedIn page that discusses and presents the job center's resources? Broken out by the total number of full-time equivalent employees at the participant's library or library system.**

| FTE Employees | Yes | No |
|---|---|---|
| Less than 10 | 0.00% | 100.00% |
| 10 to 49 | 0.00% | 100.00% |
| 50 or more | 25.00% | 75.00% |

**Table 6.10: Does the library job center have an online presence on the library's Facebook page that discusses and presents the job center's resources?**

| | Yes | No |
|---|---|---|
| Entire sample | 8.33% | 91.67% |

**Table 6.11: Does the library job center have an online presence on the library's Facebook page that discusses and presents the job center's resources? Broken out by type of library.**

| Type of Library | Yes | No |
|---|---|---|
| Central library in a system | 0.00% | 100.00% |
| Entire library system | 15.38% | 84.62% |
| Branch library | 0.00% | 100.00% |

**Table 6.12: Does the library job center have an online presence on the library's Facebook page that discusses and presents the job center's resources? Broken out by the total number of full-time equivalent employees at the participant's library or library system.**

| FTE Employees | Yes | No |
|---|---|---|
| Less than 10 | 11.11% | 88.89% |
| 10 to 49 | 0.00% | 100.00% |
| 50 or more | 12.50% | 87.50% |

**Table 6.13: Does the library job center have an online presence on the library's Google+ page that discusses and presents the job center's resources?**

| | Yes | No |
|---|---|---|
| Entire sample | 0.00% | 100.00% |

**Table 6.14: Does the library job center have an online presence on the library's YouTube page that discusses and presents the job center's resources?**

| | Yes | No |
|---|---|---|
| Entire sample | 0.00% | 100.00% |

**Are there information sources such as websites, listservs, blogs, periodicals, conferences, or other resources that you have found useful in setting up and managing your job information center? If so, what are they?**

1. Calix for local library work - other than that, it is sent to us - we haven't branched out to find any more. but we will.

2. Career coach is a member of NCDA, SHRM and ASTD professional organizations.

3. No.

4. Some WebJunction webinars have been useful. I read various library blogs to stay current, and whenever information sources are covered, I print that material and make it a part of the reference desk's "Ready Reference" file.

5. We looked at what other libraries had done, collaborated with local agencies, and asked our job seeking community to help us make our programming relevant for them.

6. Websites.

7. No.

8. Cypress press resume is new for us.

9. Websites - connected to County Job listings.

# 7. Assessment

**Has the library developed any way to assess or track how its job search efforts help library patrons? Has it developed a database of stories by patrons who found jobs through the library or made some kind of similar efforts?**

1. No but I did just have a patron who has been using the library computers to job search via WorkForce Essentials (they routed him here for the computer access. He had never touched one) and he found a job. He starts this week so I helped him print the timesheet and email from his employer about the dress code and attendance then we read over it together to make sure there was nothing else he needed to do to be prepared to start.

2. We have a shared drive file on these stories - they are anecdotal and we get their permission to share the stories with our funders.

3. No.

4. The career coach follows up with one on one clients.

5. CTC has. Yes, they're starting a monthly newsletter with success stories.

6. We have a list of the types of job related assistance provided to patrons. Most people do not come back to share if they have been successful or not. We provide them with as much information and assistance as possible, and maintain their privacy and anonymity.

7. No.

8. As we offered programming, we did do some assessment surveys and we have had stories of successful patrons told to us and shared at events.

9. We relate success stories with each other.

10. We did a survey at one point to access the usage of the library for job search. We do not have a database of stories. We have had word of mouth from patrons indicating that not only our job searching, but some of the classes we teach help them to find jobs, especially in the Microsoft office area. Many employment agencies are giving tests to see their skills, so they have been able to get them at the library.

11. No - but we've had folks email us or stop by to say thanks and let us know how they are doing.

12. None.

13. No.

14. No.

**How useful a tool would you say that your library's job center or job reference effort has been in enhancing the library's local image and obtaining funding for the future?**

1. I don't know that it is a focus for our Director but regarded as a needed service that we intend to maintain.

2. We haven't marketed it that much - but the awareness is there. More and more people are coming in for help and we are constantly busy with people looking for work.

3. The career center is small and not at all publicized. It's word of mouth, patrons are very satisfied bit visibility is low, so it doesn't enhance the library's local image much.

4. Extremely good!

5. We see this as a key strategy. We can show that our efforts help our community in many different ways. We also can show that we are community partners through our partnership with the local state-provided workforce center (Arapahoe/Douglas Works!).

6. I believe our community is aware of the helpful assistance provided by our library. In addition, many people come to the library because they have not received help elsewhere; and some come to the library knowing we have the computers and staff will be able to help them. People who have to apply online have been coming to the library for quite a while, especially those without computers or "rusty" in their computer skills.....we also help people do online applications who do not speak much English.

7. Our "Libraries for Jobseekers" Programming greatly increased the library's local image in the community; so much so that the local business association named the library director "Citizen of the Year." We are hoping that the work we have done with the business community will encourage other members of the business community to support our efforts in the future. Since our grant year ended, we have decided that each spring we will run a series of programs for job seekers and will look to the community for ways to fund these programs.

8. Our library has always been used by job seekers, even when all it offered was access to the newspaper want ads. The patrons are grateful, and job services help justify technology spending.

9. Quite important.

10. It has been a helpful alternative when other job centers are closed. It may not be funded next year because of tight budgets.

11. Good.

12. We haven't currently received funding for this issue, but we are getting data in order to look for future funding.

13. Very successful.

14. I believe we have been useful, but this has nothing to do with local funding.

15. Very useful tool.

16. Very useful.

**What advice would you give to public libraries in setting up or managing a job information center?**

1. We were able to apply for a state grant that enabled us to focus on providing this service. It has actually taken up less of our time than anticipated but collaborate with the local state agency to expand your reach and know where you are recommending your citizens too.

2. We are in the process of fighting for our existence, so I think the most important thing you can do is be focused. Despite our fight, we are moving forward with plans to expand what we offer to the public, constantly remembering who we serve and how we can help them. That is the sole reason we are here so we have to find ways to focus on our mission and serve the public in the most relevant ways.

3. Just do it. Assign specific people responsibilities and have them trained. Set up "Book a librarian" types of appointments so under-trained staff don't waste time or alienate patrons. Scan local system's efforts and collaborate on or duplicate their best practices.

4. Look for possible partnerships that already exist in your community. These kinds of partnerships are extremely beneficial for everyone. They also help to build bridges and partnerships, without wiping out the library's resources. The library does not need to be the expert, simply help to point your patrons in the right direction.

5. Space and privacy are very important; and so are the resources available for research.

6. Collaborate with any local or state agencies that offer job services to the public. Our collaboration with the Mass One Stop Career Center was invaluable. We were able to use their expertise and offer assistance to job seekers on evenings and weekends when their office was closed.

7. It's a vital service that every public library should have and promote.

8. Try to work with another local agency for trained personnel to staff your center.

9. If you are really going to get into something like this, you need to find out what the demand is, so you know where to start. Educating them on what's available before they get on the computer is the hard part. Having our computer classes on use of Excel, Word, etc. really are our greatest resources and get the best results with people looking for work. Most people just need computer knowledge.

10. Worth the effort as it bring good will back to you, your staff and the library

11. Partner with local organizations with the same goals.

12. Define a separate mission statement and a plan for implementing a job information center that fits in with your library's overall strategic plan, and then stick with that mission.

Printed in Dunstable, United Kingdom

91222490R00031